Mohandas
GANDHI

DAVID DOWNING

Heinemann Library
Chicago, Illinois

Customer Service 888-454-2279

Visit our website at www.heinemannlibrary.com

Designed by AMR
Illustrated by Art Construction
Originated by Dot Gradations
Printed in China

06 05 04 03 02
10 9 8 7 6 5 4 3 2 1

Library of Congress Cataloging-in-Publication Data

Downing, David, 1946 Aug. 9-
   Mohandas Gandhi / David Downing.
      p. cm. -- (Leading lives)
Includes bibliographical references and index.
Summary: A biography of Mahatma Gandhi, the Indian political and spiritual leader who led his country to freedom from British rule through his policy of nonviolent resistance.
   ISBN 1-58810-581-4 (lib. bdg.)   1-4034-0124-1 (pbk. bdg.)
   1. Gandhi, Mahatma, 1869-1948--Juvenile literature. 2.
Nationalists--India--Biography--Juvenile literature. 3.
Statesmen--India--Biography--Juvenile literature. [1. Gandhi, Mahatma, 1869-1948. 2. Statesmen. 3. India--Politics and government--1919-1947.]
I. Title. II. Series.
   DS481.G3 D67 2002
   954.03'5'092--dc21

                              2001003533

Acknowledgments
The publishers would like to thank the following for permission to reproduce photographs:
Popperfoto, pp. 4, 44, 47, 51; Ann and Bury Peerless, pp. 6, 52; Topham, pp. 7, 13, 20, 22, 25, 28, 34, 41, 49; Camera Press, pp. 8, 37, 55; Stone, p. 11; Hulton Archive, pp. 17, 18, 26, 29, 30, 33, 35, 43, 50; Mary Evans, p. 36.

Cover photograph reproduced with permission of Hulton Getty.

The publishers would like to thank Thames and Hudson Ltd. for permission to reproduce copyright material on p. 51.

Every effort has been made to contact copyright holders of any material reproduced in this book. Any omissions will be rectified in subsequent printings if notice is given to the publishers.

Our thanks to Christopher Gibb and Philip Emmett for their comments in the preparation of this book.

Some words are shown in bold, **like this.** You can find out what they mean by looking in the glossary.

Contents

1 A Handful of Salt

It is early April 1930. In the Indian province of Gujarat, a huge column of men and women is slowly winding its way south toward the sea.

This is no ordinary procession. For one thing, it is being watched by journalists from all around the world; for another, it contains an amazing mix of people, from poor farmers in **dhotis** to the most important leaders of India's **nationalist** movement in their tailored clothing. They are walking a road that has been watered to combat the dust and carpeted with flower petals for the bare feet of the marchers. They are walking behind a small, 60-year-old man by the name of Mohandas Gandhi.

▲ Gandhi, in the center with his chest bare, sets off from Sabarmati on his 100-mile (160-kilometer) march to the sea.

Gandhi had once studied law in London, and had been a lawyer in South Africa. He is now the British **Empire's** most dangerous opponent. Many around the world have attacked Britain's colonial system, but none before have drawn worldwide attention to its failings. Many have argued against the Empire, but few have shown it so clearly and simply for what it is—a system for the mistreatment of one people by another.

This march to the sea is a case in point. Gandhi is not leading protesters to yell violent slogans, storm police stations, or fight street battles. He is going to the beach to pick up a handful of salt. This peaceful act can hurt no one, but it happens to be illegal—only the British rulers of India have the right to India's salt. The British have decided that they, and not the citizens of India, are the only people allowed to sell India's salt. They have placed a heavy tax on salt, making it difficult for India's poor to purchase it. Salt is necessary for humans and animals to survive, especially in hot climates like India.

The world will watch as he breaks the law and demonstrates the injustice of the Empire. In a few weeks he will be arrested, but by then thousands of others will be following his example. They too will be arrested, until the prisons are bursting and the British have made themselves look foolish and mean.

The truth of India's situation will be there for all to see, and Indians, by sticking with nonviolence, will not have lowered themselves to the senseless violence of the British. On the contrary, Indian self-respect will rise as British self-respect declines, bringing both the rulers and the ruled to a new understanding of their basic equality as human beings. This will trigger the end of the Empire and the birth of an independent India. And all from a handful of salt.

2 Childhood and Youth

Mohandas Karamchand Gandhi was born in Porbandar, a white-walled city looking over the Arabian Sea, on October 2, 1869. Porbandar was a tiny, semi-independent state, one of hundreds in British-ruled India. Mohandas's father Karamchand Gandhi was its *diwan,* or leader.

▼ *This is the view from Gandhi's family home in Porbandar.*

Karamchand Gandhi was considered fair-minded, honest, and truthful, and Mohandas inherited these qualities from his father. His mother Putlibai probably influenced him even more. She was very religious—the Gandhis were **Hindus**—but Putlibai was quite willing to accept that India's other major religion, **Islam,** was an equally good way of talking to God. Both religions distinguished between right and wrong, and both encouraged people to pray, meditate, and behave better. Putlibai visited the temple every day, and often **fasted** for religious reasons. To the young Mohandas she seemed a saintly figure, and a wonderful example of a life spent in serving others.

The family shared a large, three-story house with the families of Karamchand's five brothers, so Mohandas grew up with many uncles, aunts, and cousins. He had two half-sisters from his father's earlier marriages, one older sister, Ralitabehn, and two older brothers, Lakshmidas and Karsandas.

Hinduism and caste

During Gandhi's lifetime, around 70 percent of all Indians were Hindus. Hinduism is one of the world's oldest religions, stretching back over five thousand years. It recognizes one great authority—the **Veda**—which is the source of all truth. Hindus believe in reincarnation. This means that when people die, their souls are reborn in the form of another person, plant, or animal. This happens again and again until they have learned enough to reach **salvation.**

Hindu society was divided into four **castes.** From top to bottom these are the Brahmans (priests and scholars), the Kshatriyas (warriors and rulers), the Vaisyas (merchants, traders, and farmers), and the Sudras (**artisans,** laborers, servants, and slaves). Those who did the lowest, dirtiest jobs of all were outside the four castes, and were called **Untouchables.** The Indian Constitution has since outlawed Untouchability and stated that all citizens are legally equal, but the caste system is still strong in the Indian countryside.

The young boy

Mohandas was a shy, nervous boy. Like many children, he was afraid of the dark, snakes, thieves, and ghosts. He had large ears, large eyes, and a happy smile, and from an early age he was sensitive to the suffering of others. On one occasion he climbed a mango tree to bandage fruit that he thought was "wounded." His schoolwork was inconsistent. One report found him "good at English, fair in arithmetic, and weak in geography." His conduct was good but his handwriting bad. He played **cricket** and tennis, but did not really like sports.

▶ *This photograph shows a seven-year-old Mohandas Gandhi.*

▲ Here, a teenage Gandhi (right) poses with his older brother Lakshmidas.

Gandhi was very honest. When a group of youngsters were accused of attempting to steal some bronze statues from the local temple, the six-year-old Mohandas was the only one to confess. On another occasion, a teacher who wanted to impress a visiting school inspector encouraged him to cheat on a spelling test, but Gandhi chose to ignore the hint.

Marriage and rebellion

Marriage at a young age was common in India at this time. When Mohandas was thirteen years old he married Kasturbai, also thirteen, a girl his parents had chosen for him. In later life Gandhi would campaign against child marriage, remembering how difficult he had found the first few years of his own.

Gandhi found it hard to adjust during his first months of marriage. He tried to make Kasturbai into an obedient wife and to restrict her freedom, but she refused to follow his orders. She went out on her own whenever she felt like it. Gandhi was forced to recognize that she, too, had rights, and did not need his permission to do what she wanted.

During this time, Mohandas was also learning a lot from a friend of his, Mehtab. Mehtab encouraged him to rebel against the restrictions of **Hindu** beliefs, particularly the belief held by many Hindus that eating meat was wrong. Mehtab persuaded Mohandas that the British rulers of India were strong because they ate meat, and they could only be opposed by other meat-eaters. In secret, the two friends cooked and ate a piece of goat's meat, but Mohandas soon became sick. That night he felt so guilty for eating the meat that he dreamed there was a live goat bleating in his stomach.

Once, Mohandas stole a piece of jewelry from his brother. Although he used the money to pay off his brother's debts, he felt compelled to write a letter of confession to his father. When Karamchand read the letter, he wept and embraced his son for the courage it had taken him to come forward.

Deciding his future

Around this time Karamchand became seriously ill with an ulcer. Mohandas helped care for him, sitting with him and giving him a leg massage every evening. On the day his father died, however, Mohandas was with Kasturbai. The young Gandhi never forgave himself. Kasturbai was pregnant, and when the baby died at birth Mohandas thought God was punishing him for not being at his father's side when he died.

Mohandas's family had always expected him to follow in his father's footsteps. Therefore, after finishing school at the age of seventeen, he attended college for a while in the Indian state of Gujarat. However, he did not enjoy the place or his studies there. His family then considered sending him to England where he could study to be a lawyer. Despite the birth of his first son Harilal early in the summer of 1888, he decided that this was his best option. Gandhi sailed for England on September 4, 1888, leaving Kasturbai and his infant son behind.

British India

The British first came to India as traders with the **East India Company** around 1600. At that time, the British were granted the right to trade and build factories by certain Indian leaders in exchange for providing naval protection.

Not all Indians, however, appreciated the control that the British were gaining. The British started using force to replace Indian rulers with other rulers who were loyal to the British.

In 1858, after a violent Indian revolt, **Parliament** passed an act transferring power from the East India Company to the British crown. As of that date, Britain ruled India as a conquered nation.

3 England and the Law

On the long voyage to England, Gandhi had a taste of challenges to come. The meals on the ship were difficult for him. He had no skill with a knife and fork—many Indians eat with their fingers—and the menu contained nothing for **vegetarians.** After a few days, he gave up eating in the ship's restaurant, preferring to live off the small supply of fruit and candy he had brought in his trunk. When the ship finally docked at Southampton, England, he stepped ashore in a thin, white, cotton suit, only to find that everyone else was dressed in dark, heavy clothes.

Homesick, lonely, and lacking in confidence, it took him a while to settle down. His English was not very good, and his landlady had never heard of vegetarianism. She did her best, however, feeding him porridge for breakfast, and spinach, bread, and jam for both lunch and dinner.

Fitting in

Gandhi enrolled in law school and began taking English lessons. He decided that dressing and behaving like an Englishman would help him to fit in with his classmates, so he bought new clothing. He started to take dancing lessons, common for many young men at that time, but did not feel he was very good. Speech and violin lessons followed, but proved just as unsuccessful.

▶ *Gandhi appears here dressed in the English style as a law student in London.*

Fashion victim

"He was wearing at the time a high silk top hat . . . a stiff and starched collar, a rather flashy tie displaying all the colors of the rainbow, under which there was a fine striped silk shirt. He wore as his outer clothes a morning coat [suit jacket], a double-breasted waistcoat [vest], and dark striped trousers to match, and not only patent-leather shoes but **spats** over them. He also carried leather gloves and a silver-mounted stick, but wore no spectacles. His clothes were regarded as the very acme [height] of fashion for young men about town . . . ."

(Gandhi, as described by Sachchidananda Sinha, another Indian student in London)

By chance, Gandhi found a vegetarian restaurant on London's Farringdon Street. His stomach was full for the first time since he arrived in England. He purchased a book at the restaurant called *A Plea for Vegetarianism*. This book, by author Henry Salt, helped convince him not to eat meat from that day forward.

He soon became friendly with other regular diners, most of whom were members of the **Vegetarian** Society of England. He joined the society and over the next two years wrote articles for its journal. He had found somewhere to fit in.

As a boy Gandhi had not been particularly religious, but many of his Vegetarian Society friends were interested in Indian religions.

▲ *Gandhi (sitting front left) and members of the Vegetarian Society.*

They introduced him to the epic **Hindu** poem, the ***Bhagavad Gita,*** which gave him much inspiration later in life. He also read the New Testament of the Bible, and was deeply moved by Jesus's Sermon on the Mount.

The shy lawyer

The three years went by slowly. Gandhi studied hard and explored the streets of London on long walks. He was careful with money, but managed to visit Paris in 1890 to see the new Eiffel Tower.

He cooked for friends, and occasionally played bridge, but his shyness persisted. He later said, "the presence of half a dozen or more people would strike me dumb [mute]."

Gandhi passed his law examinations on June 10, 1891, and set sail for home two days later. He arrived back in India to find that his mother had died several months earlier. Events over the next few months did little to raise his spirits. Neither his wife nor his brothers were interested in the new habits he had picked up in London, and his career as a lawyer got off to a bad start. His first legal case in Bombay ended in disaster when he felt too shy to speak up on behalf of his client. Also, his studies in London had not included **Hindu** or **Muslim** law, so Gandhi found himself at a disadvantage in his own country.

In the city of Porbandar, Gandhi's brother Lakshmidas had been fired from his job as the local ruler's secretary after arguing with a British **agent.** Gandhi had briefly met this agent in London, and Lakshmidas hoped that Gandhi could persuade the agent to give him his job back. Gandhi did not want to use his connections, but reluctantly agreed to try. The agent thought that Gandhi had overstepped his bounds as an Indian, and threw him out of his office.

He later claimed that this incident changed the entire path of his life. It clearly showed him the great unfairness of living under British colonial rule. Indians were not permitted to live freely or control their own lives. That was left to their British rulers. When Gandhi received an offer from the Muslim Indian firm of Dada Abdullah to represent them in a South African legal dispute, he was happy to accept. Expecting to be away for less than a year, he left his family behind once more.

4 Birth of a Rebel

Soon after arriving in South Africa (see the map on page 16), Gandhi arranged a business meeting in Transvaal, the capital city of Pretoria. He bought a first-class ticket for the journey from Durban, but when the train reached Maritzburg a white passenger took one look at Gandhi in the first-class compartment and angrily fetched the officials. They told Gandhi that only white people were allowed to travel first class. When he refused to travel in third class, they made him get off the train. He spent the whole night on the freezing Maritzburg platform, angry about the injustice he had suffered.

Should he give up and go home to India? Should he forget about the train incident and carry on with the legal case? Or should he stay and fight for justice, for himself, and his fellow Indians? He decided to fight. It was, he later said, one of the defining moments of his life.

His northward journey continued to be eventful. One portion was by stagecoach, and the conductor insisted that Gandhi sit next to the driver rather than ride in comfort inside. Later, when the conductor wanted to sit outside and get some fresh air, he demanded that Gandhi perch on the footboard. When Gandhi refused, he dragged him off the coach and beat him until the other passengers intervened.

In Johannesburg, Gandhi was not allowed into the Grand National Hotel. On the train to Pretoria, however, an Englishman stood up for him when another conductor tried to have him ejected from the first-class compartment. This, and similar support from white guests in his Pretoria hotel, encouraged him. Many whites obviously felt that **racial discrimination** was wrong.

Gandhi's South Africa

In May 1893, when Gandhi's boat arrived in Durban, the area now known as South Africa was still a mixture of British colonies (Cape Colony and Natal), independent **Boer** republics (Transvaal and the Orange Free State), and loosely defined tribal areas. The population of the whole area was made of around two million Africans, 500,000 European settlers, and roughly 80,000 Indians. About half the Indians were **indentured laborers,** people who had come from India to work on farms owned by settlers for a five-year period. They were paid next to nothing, and had virtually no rights. The remaining Indians were tradesmen, **artisans,** and professionals like Gandhi.

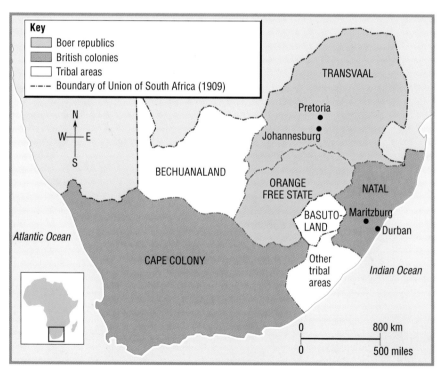

▲ This map shows South Africa in Gandhi's time.

No ordinary rebel

All these negative experiences had affected Gandhi, and shortly after his arrival in Pretoria he called a meeting of all the Indians in the city. He discovered, to his surprise, that the events of the past week had cured him of his shyness as a public speaker. He told the audience about his recent experiences and listened to those of other Indians: they could not own land or vote, they could not stay outside after 9:00 p.m. without a permit, and they weren't allowed to use the sidewalks during the day.

What could they do about all this? An ordinary rebel would have simply protested against the actions taken by those in power, but Gandhi was not an ordinary rebel. He told the other Indians that they must first show themselves worthy of equality. They must clean up their neighborhoods, learn to speak English (which Gandhi offered to teach them), and always be honest in their business deals. **Hindus** and **Muslims** must respect and get along with each other. Then they could demand equality with a good conscience.

In the meantime, Gandhi helped bring about an agreement in the case he had been hired to handle. The agreement saved both sides a lot of time and money, and this was the way that Gandhi tried to solve all his cases for the rest of the time he practiced law. With the case successfully closed, he could look forward to returning to India.

▶ *Here, Gandhi sits outside his Johannesburg law office in 1905. Henry Polak (standing at left) and Gandhi's secretary, Sonya Schlesin (seated at right), were two of his earliest non-Indian supporters.*

YOU CAN FIND THE PLACES GANDHI TRAVELED IN SOUTH AFRICA ON THE MAP ON PAGE 16.

Making himself unpopular

Then, at a farewell party in Durban, Gandhi discovered that the Government of Natal was about to take voting rights away from the few Indians who had them. This must be resisted, he told his friends. They begged him to stay and lead the resistance. He agreed to postpone his departure for a month.

He organized a 10,000-signature **petition** to be sent to the colonial secretary in London, and set up the **Natal Indian Congress** to campaign for Indian rights. He stressed that this was not just a political struggle, not just about changing government policies; it was also an educational struggle that was meant to change the way people thought.

A matter of rights

"I discovered that as a man and as an Indian I had no rights. More correctly, I discovered that I had no rights as a man because I was an Indian."

(Gandhi, speaking in South Africa)

The month became a year and Gandhi, realizing that he would probably be in South Africa for longer, went home to India to collect Kasturbai and his two sons. Their ship, which was also carrying hundreds of Indian immigrants, reached Durban late in December 1896, but it was mid-January before they were allowed to dock. The officials were reluctant to allow so many new immigrants ashore, and they were particularly angry with Gandhi, whose speeches in India criticizing the South African authorities had been reported in the press. Eventually Kasturbai and the children were smuggled ashore, but Gandhi himself was caught by a white mob and kicked and punched. He might have been severely injured had the local police chief's wife not intervened quickly. She got him to the house of an Indian merchant, and, when this was found by the mob, Gandhi escaped out the back.

It was a shocking introduction to South Africa for Kasturbai, and there were more shocks in store. Over the last few years Gandhi had been simplifying his lifestyle. His law practice had made him rich, but he insisted on cutting his own hair and doing his own laundry so that he could spend more money to help the poor. His house was full of strangers, some of whom, to Kasturbai's horror, turned out to be **Untouchables.** They argued long and hard about this, and it would be years before she came to accept his unusual ways of living. Over the next three years she gave birth to two more sons: Ramdas in 1897 and Devadas in 1900.

War

In 1899, the **Second Boer War** broke out between Britain and the two Boer republics of Transvaal and the Orange Free State. Gandhi supported the British, arguing that because he was demanding rights from the **Empire** he had a duty to help it. His offer to form an Indian ambulance unit was eventually accepted, and he and many others received medals for their brave service. Their loyal involvement in the war changed the way South Africa's Indians were seen by the British in England, and in 1901, Gandhi felt able to take his family back to India.

▶ *British soldiers, right, cross a river during the Boer War.*

Loyalty to one's government

"Every single subject of a state must not hope to enforce his opinion in all cases. The authorities may not always be right, but as long as the subjects owe allegiance to a state, it is their clear duty generally to accommodate themselves, and to accord their support, to the acts of the state."

(Gandhi as quoted by Louis Fischer in his 1950 book *The Life of Mahatma Gandhi*)

▲ *Gandhi's Indian Ambulance Corps is pictured during the Boer War.*

Back in India, in 1901, Gandhi attended an **Indian National Congress (INC)** meeting for the first time in Calcutta. He was eager to renew **nationalist** contacts made during his visit in 1896, but many participants seemed more concerned with upholding **caste** status, arguing that only **Untouchables** should clean bathrooms. Gandhi set an example of equality among **Hindus** by picking up a mop and bucket himself.

He set up a new law practice in Bombay, but the business was only a few months old when he received an urgent summons from the Indian community in South Africa. The gains he had helped to make had been lost, and he was needed again.

A simpler life

When Gandhi returned he found that Indians were being treated worse in Transvaal than in Natal, so Gandhi decided to establish his home and law practice in Johannesburg, where a mass protest meeting was to be held. He started a newspaper, *Indian Opinion*, early in 1903 to cover the affairs of the Indian community. This was printed over 400 miles (640 kilometers) away in Durban, and Gandhi often had to make the day-long journey by train. On one such trip, he read a book that profoundly influenced him for the rest of his life: *Unto This Last* by John Ruskin. Ruskin argued that the more an individual gave to society, the more he or she personally gained. He stressed that all individuals were equally valuable members of the human race: for example, barbers were just as important as lawyers. He also believed a life of manual labor was the most fulfilling life.

Ruskin's arguments fitted in with his own beliefs, and encouraged Gandhi to change his life. The *Indian Opinion* office was moved to a 99-acre (40-hectare) plot of land 14 miles (22 kilometers) outside Durban, and homes were built for the workers and their families.

YOU CAN FIND THE PLACES GANDHI TRAVELED IN SOUTH AFRICA ON THE MAP ON PAGE 16.

21

Phoenix Farm, as the new settlement was called, was meant to be a **self-sufficient commune,** where everyone could grow their own food and earn the same wages.

For the next few years, Gandhi divided his time between the farm and his law practice in Johannesburg. During this time he read and talked a lot about religion. He befriended a group of **Quakers,** and studied both the Bible and the Koran, the holy book of **Islam.** He thought that the problem with Christianity was its failure to love and respect all living things. The main problem with **Hinduism,** he thought, was the appalling treatment of the **Untouchables** and the **caste** system.

He continued to simplify his life. According to the *Bhagavad Gita,* material possessions made it harder to reap **spiritual** rewards, so Gandhi gave most of his away. Also, to help himself focus on what he felt was important in life, he took a **vow** of **celibacy** in 1906 at age 37, as many religious figures do. He began to **fast,** and also gave up his house in Johannesburg.

▲ *Members of Phoenix Farm, the commune in South Africa where Gandhi lived and worked, posed for this photograph in 1906.*

Satyagraha

Later that same year the Transvaal authorities, now under **Boer** control, proposed and passed a new law requiring Indians—and only Indians—to register, have their fingerprints taken, and carry passes at all times. This was a clear case of **racial discrimination,** and Gandhi called a protest meeting in September 1906. Thousands of Indians attended. When one man passionately promised to take a vow of resistance, Gandhi pointed out how important it was to take such vows seriously. The consequences of such disobedience, he pointed out, would probably include threats, beatings, and prison. The audience did not care. They all swore to resist the new law.

A mystery

"It has always been a mystery to me how men can feel themselves honored by the humiliation of their fellow beings."

(Gandhi, speaking in South Africa)

Gandhi's strategy for the campaign was simple. They would ignore the new rules and, if threatened with violence, refuse to fight back. The protesters did not need the force of violence because they already had *satyagraha*—the "force of truth"—on their side. The *satyagrahis,* as he called the nonviolent protesters, should never forget that it was evil they were fighting, not individuals. They should always treat people with courtesy. Indeed, in the years to come, Gandhi nearly always sent his opponents a polite warning when action was imminent.

The campaign went well. Only a few hundred of the 13,000 Indians in Transvaal registered under the new law, and the authorities responded by arresting Gandhi and other prominent leaders. It was his first time in jail.

This achieved nothing, so General Jan Smuts, the official in charge of Indian affairs, offered to release the prisoners and abandon the new law if the Indians would only agree to register voluntarily. Gandhi accepted the deal: a *satyagrahi* had to trust his opponent, whether or not the opponent deserved trust.

Smuts did not. The law was not repealed, and Gandhi led 2,000 protesters in burning their certificates of registration. He and many others, including his son Harilal, were rearrested. The campaign went on.

Tolstoy Farm

In prison, Gandhi read two more books that deepened and reinforced his convictions: Henry Thoreau's *Civil Disobedience* and Leo Tolstoy's *The Kingdom of God Is Within You.* He started writing to Tolstoy, a successful Russian author who had given away his possessions, given up tobacco, alcohol, and meat, and adopted a simpler life on a farm.

When Gandhi was released he borrowed money from a German friend and used it to set up another **commune,** this time in the Transvaal, that he called Tolstoy Farm. It was intended partly as a refuge for released and penniless *satyagrahis* and partly as another experiment in living. The residents built their own homes, grew their own food, and made their own clothes. Gandhi baked bread, made marmalade, and taught the children. He began to **fast** regularly during this period, believing that this cleared his mind and purified his soul. His diet was now restricted to fruit, nuts, olive oil, and cereal.

◀ *Gandhi's wife Kasturbai is shown here with their four sons. From left to right they are Harilal, Ramdas, Devadas, and Manilal. This photo was taken in South Africa in 1902.*

Victory in South Africa

The registration issue simmered for several years, before being submerged in a wider dispute. First, it was announced that former **indentured laborers** would have to continue paying a high tax simply to stay in South Africa. Secondly, new measures were introduced to restrict Indian movement between the provinces. Finally, in 1913, the highest court in South Africa refused to recognize non-Christian marriages—such as Indian marriages—that were not registered with the government. The Indian community was outraged, and Gandhi launched a new *satyagraha* campaign.

The campaign lasted over a year, and ended in at least a partial victory. The arrest and imprisonment of thousands of Indians alarmed some politicians in London and India, and they pressured the South African government to change these policies. This seemed to put the Indians in a strong position, but when a strike by white South African miners further weakened the government's position, Gandhi called off the campaign. It was not right, he said, to profit from others' troubles. Smuts and the other South African leaders were so impressed by this that they agreed to abolish the tax, to recognize all marriages, and to stop the arrival of all indentured laborers from India by 1920.

In July 1914, Gandhi finally left South Africa for the last time. "The saint has left our shores," Jan Smuts said, "I hope forever."

◀ South Africa's minister in charge of Indian affairs, Jan Christian Smuts, considered Gandhi a worthy opponent.

A more than worthy opponent

Just before leaving South Africa, Gandhi gave his secretary a pair of sandals he had made in prison and asked that they be given to General Smuts as a gesture of esteem. Smuts wore the sandals every summer while at his farm. "I have worn these sandals for many a summer since then," Smuts wrote many years later, "even though I may feel that I am not worthy to stand in the shoes of so great a man."

Smuts returned the sandals to Gandhi in 1939 for Gandhi's 70th birthday as a sign of respect.

6 Homecoming

Gandhi arrived in England on August 6, 1914, soon after **World War I** broke out, and his offer to form another Indian ambulance corps was accepted. In December he and his family set sail for India, from which he had been gone for ten years, and during the long voyage he must have thought a great deal about his country and his own role in influencing its future.

In 1909 Gandhi had written a pamphlet called *Hind Swaraj,* or *Indian Home Rule*, in which he had argued for a semi-independent India within the **Empire.** Although this seemed progressive, some of his other recommendations—a return to small-scale **cottage industry,** the abolition of the railways, and the maintenance of **caste**—seemed less so. How would he be received in his own country? On arrival, he visited the old **nationalist** leader Gokhale, whom he had already met on several occasions. Gokhale told Gandhi to take a good long look at India, and to keep his ears open and his mouth shut for a whole year.

Sabarmati

Gandhi took the advice. For a year he crisscrossed India, talking and listening to people, always traveling third class. He no longer wore European clothes, just a simple *dhoti* and cap. He spoke English only when it was absolutely necessary.

India in the early twentieth century

The growth of administration and business in the late nineteenth and early twentieth centuries had contributed to the creation of a small and often English-educated Indian middle class. The vast majority of Indians, however, still lived in villages that lacked the most basic services, like running water or a road to the outside world. Since the early 1800s, the British had been promising the Indians that they would be able to participate more in politics, but in 1915 they still held only five percent of the posts in the **Indian Civil Service.**

YOU CAN FIND THE PLACES GANDHI TRAVELED IN INDIA ON THE MAP ON PAGE 40.

The India that Gandhi found made him think. So many things were neglected and filthy: train compartments, temples, even the sacred Ganges River at Benares. The **Untouchables** were still living off others' rubbish.

He decided to lead by example, as he had in South Africa, and established an *ashram* at Sabarmati in his native Gujarat. Gandhi's own room at the *ashram* was no larger than a cell, with a small terrace outside, on which he slept and worked. He started to wear only Indian clothing, and began to look upon all Indians as members of his family. The residents agreed to live by the same principles of **self-sufficiency** and nonviolence, to stress cleanliness, and to forego meat and alcohol. They also **vowed** to reject the **caste** system, but when Gandhi admitted a family of Untouchables some people left the *ashram* in protest and its financial sponsors withdrew their support. Gandhi was wondering how the community was going to survive when a sympathetic **Muslim** drove up one day, opened the window, and handed over a bundle of money.

Family life

His relationship with Kasturbai had slowly grown closer over the years. She still sometimes did not agree with him, but was more inclined to listen to his ideas, particularly now that so many other people looked up to him.

▶ *Gandhi and Kasturbai are pictured here on their return to India in early 1915.*

28

Gandhi was less successful as a father, particularly with his older sons Harilal and Manilal. He expected them to behave like independent adults, but refused to let them make their own decisions, particularly where marriage partners were concerned. Harilal ended up as an alcoholic who did his best to shame his father; Manilal was sent back to South Africa for most of the next 25 years to edit *Indian Opinion*. Devadas and Ramdas were only teenagers at this time, and benefited from Gandhi becoming more tolerant as he grew older.

Speaking out

In early 1916, Gandhi was invited to speak at the opening of the **Hindu** University in Benares. He used the occasion to express his concerns. India was enslaved, poor, dirty, and uneducated, he said. He went on to say that there would be no real hope for the country until the people in the well-dressed audience gave up their jewelry. His speech was interrupted by angry shouts. Many walked out in protest.

▲ *This is the holy city of Benares, now called Varanasi, where Gandhi addressed the Hindu University on February 6, 1916.*

Gandhi took a similar message to the annual meeting of the **INC** in Lucknow. It would be the farmers that would save India, Gandhi said, not the lawyers, doctors, and other professionals who had previously made up the **nationalist** movement.

Gandhi felt that without the farmers, independence would just be a matter of handing power from the British ruling class to the Indian middle class. India would then, he thought, follow Britain down the road of **industrialism** and **materialism.** Real independence would involve more than that. India would need to follow its own, more **spiritual** path.

Champaran

In 1915, the Indian poet Tagore had publicly called Gandhi a *mahatma*, or "great soul," and by the end of 1916 Gandhi's growing reputation as a defender of the poor encouraged many to ask for his help. One farmer was particularly persistent, following Gandhi around until he agreed to visit the

Champaran district, where **indigo** farmers were in dispute with their English landlords. Gandhi quickly discovered that the landlords were indeed demanding excessive rents, and that the lawyers the farmers had hired to help them were just as dishonest.

◀ *The Indian writer and philosopher Rabindranath Tagore, at left, gave Gandhi the name* mahatma, *meaning "great soul."*

Gandhi was arrested by the local administration because of his plan to help the farmers, but the **viceroy** in Delhi feared that this would cause trouble. He therefore ordered that Gandhi be released. Gandhi then went on to hear the complaints of 7,000 farmers, and to put together a convincing case on their behalf. The landlords were forced to admit they had been wrong, and were made to pay back at least some of the excessive rents they had charged.

Home rule?

World War I was now nearing its end. Gandhi hoped that when peace came, the British would grant the Indians some measure of **home rule** in exchange for the loyalty they had shown during the war. He was disappointed. The British, instead of introducing home rule, took a harder line with Indian nationalism. Gandhi knew the nationalists had to respond, but how?

Saying no
"What I did was a very ordinary thing. I declared that the British could not order me about in my own country."
(Gandhi, on his actions in Champaran)

7 Noncooperation

On March 18, 1919, the **Rowlatt Bills** were signed into law. They introduced, among other things, imprisonment without trial. That night, the idea of a nationwide **hartal,** or general strike, came to Gandhi in a dream. On the chosen day no one would go to work and no shops would open. India would grind to a halt for one day, and after that a *satyagraha* campaign would unfold according to circumstances.

YOU CAN FIND THE SITES OF GANDHI'S CAMPAIGNS ON THE MAP ON PAGE 40.

The *hartal* was fixed for March 30, but then changed to April 6. In Delhi, however, it went ahead on the original March date. Government troops fired on one peaceful demonstration, killing nine people, and in the days that followed there were violent revolts. The nationwide event on April 6, though peaceful in most places, also led to violent disturbances in the Punjab. When Gandhi was prevented from reaching Delhi by the British, the trouble spread still further. Trains were blocked, shops looted, and government offices burned down.

The Indian people, Gandhi decided, were not yet ready for the self-discipline of a *satyagraha* campaign. He had made a mistake.

The Amritsar Massacre
Gandhi was not the only one to make a mistake. In the Punjabi city of Amritsar the *hartal* passed peacefully, but that peace would not last. On April 12, a proclamation was issued that prohibited Indians from marching or meeting together, but it was not posted in many parts of the city. On April 13, a peaceful meeting of unarmed Indians in an enclosed square, the Jallianwalla Bagh, was attacked by the troops of the British General Dyer. The Indians were given no warning. Dyer reported to his superior that he was trying to teach the Indians a lesson. The shooting went on for ten minutes. When it was over 379 were dead and 1,137 wounded.

▲ *This still from the film* Gandhi *shows British troops firing on the unarmed demonstrators at Amritsar.*

Mass murder

Hunter Commission: "From time to time you changed your firing and directed it to the place where the crowd was thickest?"

General Dyer: "That is so."

Hunter Commission: "Supposing the passage [the entrance to the square] was sufficient to allow the armored cars to go in, would you have opened fire with the machine guns?"

General Dyer: "I think, probably, yes."

> (General Dyer replying to questions from members of the Hunter Commission, which was set up by the British government to investigate the Amritsar Massacre)

The lesson Indians learned was the opposite of what was intended. "When a government takes up arms against its unarmed subjects then it has forfeited the right to govern," Gandhi said, and few, if any, Indians disagreed with him. The British still had the power to rule India, but any lingering belief in their right to rule died in the dust of the Jallianwalla Bagh.

Two struggles

Gandhi's next move, in November 1919, was to announce a policy of **noncooperation** with British rule. This meant that Indians did not take their legal problems to British courts, and Indian soldiers refused to serve in the British Army. Indians also stopped buying imported British goods, which meant that industries in Britain lost money. Gandhi sent back the medal he had won in the **Boer War** and organized a national volunteer corps to spread the idea of noncooperation throughout the country.

Enormous amounts of imported British cloth were burned in ceremonial bonfires. If Indians spun their own cloth, Gandhi said, they could both challenge the British and assert their own independence in a peaceful and positive way. The spinning wheel, or *charkha,* became the symbol of Indian **nationalism** at that time.

▲ *These people in Delhi in the early 1920s are demonstrating their support for Gandhi.*

Gandhi took more interest in the **INC,** which he decided should serve as a nationwide school for teaching the principles of *satyagraha.* In 1920, he rewrote the INC's constitution, making it possible for anyone to join by paying a small sum of money. Now the poor majority of India's population could contribute to the two parallel struggles that Gandhi believed Indians were engaged in: the eviction of the British and the renewal of India.

Chauri Chaura

The campaign of noncooperation continued through 1920 and 1921, with increasing social disruptions. Thousands were arrested, including Gandhi, but the campaign went on. When the **Prince of Wales** visited India in 1921, he paraded through empty streets: almost no one came to see him.

British treatment of Indians grew increasingly brutal: the number of beatings rose sharply, both inside and outside the overflowing prisons. However, the British showed no signs of changing their policies, and the INC decided to change their actions from noncooperation to outright nonviolent **civil disobedience.** The original plan was to mount the campaign throughout India, but Gandhi persuaded the other leaders to restrict it to one area: Bardoli.

The campaign had barely started when news arrived in February 1922 of an atrocity 800 miles (1,280 kilometers) away in the small town of Chauri Chaura. A group of Indian policemen who had fired on Indian demonstrators had been hacked to pieces by a Nationalist mob.

A shocked Gandhi called off all active resistance to the British. The events at Chauri Chaura, he said, showed "the way India may easily go, if drastic precautions are not taken." The Indian people, Gandhi thought, were still not ready for true independence.

▶ *Gandhi and his wife Kasturbai are pictured here in 1922.*

Gandhi's abandonment of the campaign was not popular with many of his supporters, and the British took the opportunity to arrest and try him for **sedition** on March 10, 1922. **"Noncooperation** with evil is as much a duty as is cooperation with good," he told the court, but he made no attempt to deny his involvement. On the contrary, he asked for the most severe punishment possible. The judge reluctantly sentenced him to six years, adding that if the government decided to reduce the term, "no one would be better pleased than I."

Gandhi served less than two years in Yeravda Prison. Unlike most Indian prisoners, Gandhi was treated fairly well. He had time to meditate, to read and write, to pray, and to spin cloth. His real punishment was the loss of his freedom: he was not able to travel the country as he had been doing, and not able to see first-hand what was happening.

In January 1924, however, he developed appendicitis, and had to have an operation. His recovery was slow and the British, fearing he might die in their custody, hurried to release him. They did not want to be blamed for his death.

◀ *Gandhi is shown here at his spinning wheel. He encouraged Indians to make their own cloth instead of using expensive, imported British cloth.*

Hindus and Muslims

While recuperating near Bombay, Gandhi learned from other **INC** leaders what had happened during his time in jail. The noncooperation movement had, for the moment, died. More seriously for the long term, the cooperation between **Hindus** and **Muslims,** widespread in 1918 and 1919, had been replaced by growing mistrust. Violent **intercommunal** riots were becoming more frequent.

Gandhi believed that Indian independence was impossible without cooperation between the Hindus and Muslims—he thought they needed to present a united front to the British—and he took dramatic action to unite the split. In September 1924, he announced that he would undertake a 21-day **fast** in support of friendship between the two communities. He was now 55 years old, and had not yet fully recovered from his operation. As his fast progressed, the nation held its breath. One by one, Hindu and Muslim leaders pledged to live in brotherhood.

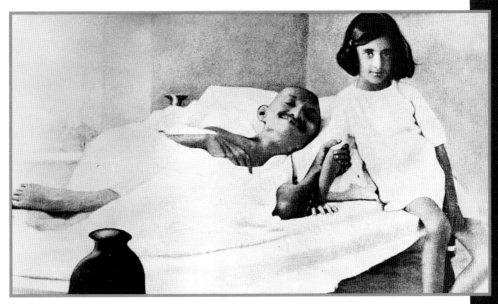

▲ Gandhi is pictured recovering from a fast in 1924 in the company of Indira, the six-year-old daughter of Jawaharlal Nehru (an important member of the Indian National Congress). She eventually married another, unrelated, Gandhi, and became **prime minister** of India as Indira Gandhi in 1966.

A political guru

Gandhi made no attempt to revive **noncooperation;** the time, he felt, was not right. He concentrated instead on preparing his country for the future. He resigned from the political leadership of the **INC** and for the next five years divided his time between travel around India and the *ashram* at Sabarmati. Kasturbai usually stayed at the *ashram*, but sons Ramdas and Devadas often accompanied their father during his travels.

On his journeys through the villages Gandhi argued for **Hindu–Muslim** unity, spoke against the **caste** system, (staying in the homes of **Untouchables** whenever he could), and encouraged everyone to spin cloth each day. He preached the virtues of **self-sufficiency** and hygiene, and discouraged the use of alcohol and drugs. He promoted both the equality of women and the use of Hindustani, an Indian language, as an alternative to English. He also supplied useful amateur medical advice. In the rare moments he had to himself he would read and write letters.

At the *ashram* life was simpler and less tiring. Gandhi was the natural leader, but he peeled potatoes and did his chores like everyone else. He was strict about punctuality, cleanliness, not wasting money, and spinning cloth daily, but when it came to ideas and beliefs he was very tolerant. There were many long-term visitors to the *ashram* who did not share his faith in God, his friendship with Muslims, or his belief in nonviolence. He argued pleasantly with them all.

Gandhi's quick wit was legendary. When a doctor told him that if all sick people simply went to bed they would get better, he replied: "Don't say that out loud—you'll lose all your patients."

A year's warning

Early in 1928, a group of politicians—called the Simon Commission—was sent from Great Britain to study conditions in British India and make recommendations for political reform. The British expected the Indians to be pleased, but the Indians were enraged by the fact that the Simon Commission contained not one single Indian. An almost unanimous decision was made by **Nationalists** not to cooperate with the commission in any way, and in February 1928 Gandhi announced the beginning of a new *satyagraha* campaign against British tax increases in the Bardoli region.

The year 1928 was full of turmoil. As the new *satyagraha* campaign gathered strength, the travels of the Simon Commission sparked protests and riots. Many Indians were arrested. The government was forced to scale back the tax increases in Bardoli, but Gandhi, remembering the violence of earlier years, was reluctant to mount a nationwide campaign. He agreed with the other INC leaders to give the British a year's warning: if they did not grant India **dominion status** by the end of 1929, then Gandhi would lead a nonviolent campaign against them.

March to the sea

In October 1929, with that deadline fast approaching, the **Viceroy** Lord Irwin announced that India would eventually be given dominion status. The Indians felt that was too little, too late. On January 1, 1930, Jawaharlal Nehru, the newly elected president of the INC, proclaimed India's declaration of independence. The country waited for Gandhi to make his first move in a new campaign of **civil disobedience.**

Two months later, on March 12, Gandhi set off from Sabarmati with 70 members of the **ashram** and walked south toward the sea to gather salt. The **viceroy** and several **INC** leaders had laughed when they heard of his plan, but it became the most effective of all Gandhi's **satyagraha** demonstrations.

▼ *This is India as it was in Gandhi's time.*

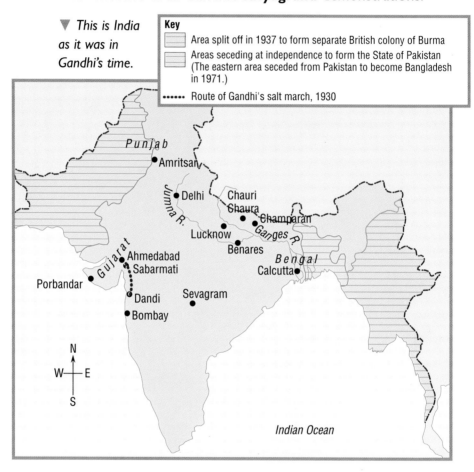

Key

Area split off in 1937 to form separate British colony of Burma

Areas seceding at independence to form the State of Pakistan (The eastern area seceded from Pakistan to become Bangladesh in 1971.)

•••••• Route of Gandhi's salt march, 1930

Punjab
●Amritsar

Jumna R.
●Delhi Chauri Chaura
●Champaran
●Lucknow Ganges R.
●Benares
●Ahmedabad *Bengal*
●Sabarmati Calcutta●
Porbandar *Gujarat*
Dandi Sevagram ●
●Bombay

N
W—E
S

Indian Ocean

All Indians understood the importance of salt for humans and animals in a hot climate, and the British control of and tax on salt seemed as unreasonable as a tax on air or water would have been. When Gandhi and his followers reached the coast at Dandi a month later, the whole nation was watching. In the weeks after he picked up his illegal handful of salt from the beach, 100,000 Indians—including Gandhi's sons Manilal,

Ramdas, and Devadas—went to prison for following his example. These imprisonments only drove the lesson home: British rule was unjust, unnecessary, and unwanted. The entire world began to feel this way when Gandhi's followers marched on the Dharasana salt factories in 1930, and Indian policemen proceeded to beat the unarmed marchers without mercy.

The British held a meeting on the future of India in November 1930, but with all the INC leaders in prison there was no chance of progress. London politicians reluctantly informed Lord Irwin that he would have to make a deal with Gandhi.

▲ *Here, Gandhi breaks British tax laws by picking up a handful of natural salt at Dandi, on the west coast of India.*

Dharasana

"In complete silence, the Gandhi men drew up and halted a hundred yards from the stockade. A picked column advanced from the crowd, waded the ditches, and approached the barbed wire stockade . . . . Suddenly, at a word of command, scores of native policemen rushed upon the advancing marchers and rained blows on their heads with their steel-shod **lathis.** Not one of the marchers even raised an arm to fend off the blows. They went down like ten-pins. From where I stood I heard the sickening whack of the clubs on unprotected skulls . . . ."

(American journalist Webb Miller, observing *satyagraha* in action at the Dharasana Saltworks, where two demonstrators were killed and hundreds wounded on May 21, 1930)

Early in 1931, Gandhi and **Viceroy** Lord Irwin met eight times. The agreement they reached was called the Delhi Pact. In return for Gandhi calling off the *satyagraha* campaign, Irwin promised to release all prisoners, return property taken from Indians, and allow the collection of salt from India's beaches. There was no talk of independence, but that would be discussed by a second meeting later in the year.

Fall from grace

"[England] is no longer regarded as the champion throughout the world of fair dealing and the exponent of high principle, but as the upholder of Western race supremacy and the exploiter of those outside her own borders."

(Indian poet Rabindranath Tagore, speaking to the *Manchester Guardian* in May 1930)

Some British people welcomed this apparent softening of their government's attitude, but one well-known political figure did not. Winston Churchill (who later became **prime minister** of the United Kingdom), commenting on Gandhi's meetings with Irwin, spoke of "the nauseating and humiliating spectacle of this one-time . . . lawyer, now **seditious** *fakir,* striding half-naked up the steps of the viceroy's palace, there to **negotiate** . . . on equal terms with the representative of the **King-Emperor.**"

Not all Gandhi's enemies were British. Many members of India's minority communities, particularly the **Muslims** and **Untouchables**, thought the **Hindus** might prove to be worse rulers than the British. The leaders of these minority communities were determined to safeguard their rights before independence was granted. Before leaving for London, Gandhi reluctantly accepted a **separate electorate** for Muslims. Only this, the Muslims thought, would ensure that their voices would be heard in the government of an independent India.

England

Accompanied by his son Devadas, Gandhi left to attend meetings in London at the end of August and stayed in England for 84 days. On a personal level his visit was a huge success. His hosts had provided him with a luxuriant suite at the Ritz Hotel, but he chose instead to stay at a community center in the poverty-stricken neighborhood of London's East End. He strode out every morning ahead of his exhausted police escort and talked to everyone he met. The children called him Uncle Gandhi.

During his time in England Gandhi met several famous people, including the film comedian Charlie Chaplin and ex-Prime Minister Lloyd George, and was invited to Buckingham Palace for tea with the king and queen. When a reporter asked Gandhi if he had worn enough clothes for the occasion, he replied that the king had been wearing enough for both of them!

▼ *Gandhi is shown here surrounded by employees of a Lancashire mill.*

43

He addressed several meetings, spent two weekends at Oxford University talking with professors, and visited a Lancashire textile mill that had been badly affected by the Indian boycotts of British cloth. At the end of one meeting, a worker announced: "I am one of the unemployed, but if I was in India I would say the same thing that Mr. Gandhi is saying." Everywhere Gandhi went, people admired him.

Deadlock

Gandhi's meeting with the British government was much less successful. The government was reluctant to make any definite promises about reform, and various other Indian groups now shared the **Muslim** desire for **separate electorates.** Gandhi hated this idea: he wanted Indians to rise above their divisions, not give in to them. When the conference ended Gandhi said "I have come back empty-handed, but I have not compromised the honor of my country."

▼ *This photo was taken of Gandhi at his meeting with the British government in September 1931. The man sitting to his left, Pandit Malaviya, is one of his colleagues.*

Two days after he returned to India, Gandhi was arrested without charge or trial. Lord Willingdon, Irwin's less knowledgeable successor as **viceroy,** was determined to make certain that there would be no new campaign following the failure of the conference. The **INC** was outlawed and soon 35,000 of its members were behind bars.

While in prison, Gandhi worried about the divisions among Indians. He was particularly concerned about the **Untouchables,** who now had their own organization led by Bhimrao Ambedkar. When the British agreed to separate electorates for the Untouchables in regional elections, Gandhi was appalled. He understood the Untouchables' concern—few Indians were as ready to accept them as he was—but he was convinced that segregation—a forced separation—was not the answer. On September 20, 1932, he started a **fast** unto death against the decision.

Children of God

Gandhi was 63 years old now, and by the fourth day of the fast his doctors were seriously worried. All of India held its breath as various political leaders desperately sought the compromise that would save him. On the sixth day they found it: the separate electorates would be a purely temporary measure. On the seventh day, Gandhi allowed Kasturbai to bring him a glass of orange juice.

The political deal was only a small part of the story. Gandhi's fast had inspired people all over India to open their temples to those they called Untouchables, and whom he called *harijans,* or "children of God." Prominent people accepted food from *harijan* hands, and hundreds of villages decided to let *harijans* use their wells. The "scourge of **Hinduism,**" as Gandhi had called untouchability, had received a serious blow.

Gandhi was released from prison in May 1933. His critics could claim that after four years of protest and **negotiation,** India had still not achieved independence or the promise of it. But independence was nearer, and so, in Gandhi's mind, was a better India. He had no use for one without the other.

On the road

While Gandhi was in prison, the British had decided to tax the thriving Sabarmati *ashram.* When the residents refused to pay, their money, goods, and property were seized. After his release Gandhi ordered the abandonment of the *ashram*, telling his followers to spread themselves across the villages of India.

In 1934 he resigned his seat in the **INC,** confident that his friend Jawaharlal Nehru could handle the political side of things while he concentrated on reforming India. For most of the next six years he crossed India on foot, like a wandering *sadhu* (holy man). In village after village he promoted small-scale industry and repeated his familiar messages of religious tolerance and love. In 1936, he established a new *ashram* at Sevagram in central India. Kasturbai and Gandhi, very close partners during this period, came to consider Sevagram home.

Pakistan

In the political world there was some progress toward independence. The 1935 India Act offered Indians a measure of self-rule, but real power remained with the British. Gandhi commented that India was still a prison, but that the inmates were now allowed to elect their jailers. Despite this, the INC agreed to contest the new elections, and won majorities in nine of India's eleven provinces.

▲ *Gandhi (at right) sits with Indian politician Jawaharlal Nehru. The two men disagreed on many things, but they loved and trusted each other.*

Significantly, the **Muslim League** won only five percent of the **Muslim** vote. Its leader, Mohammed Jinnah, was desperate to remain in power. He fueled Muslim fears of **Hindu** rule and focused those fears into calls for an independent Muslim country of Pakistan. The scene was set for the final round of India's fight for independence.

Two Gandhian thoughts

"**Caste** has nothing to do with religion in general and Hinduism in particular. It is a sin to believe anyone else is inferior or superior to ourselves."

"Religions are different roads converging to the same point. What does it matter that we take different roads as long as we reach the same goal. In reality, there are as many different religions as there are individuals."

10 A Light in the Darkness

When **World War II** broke out in September 1939, the British **viceroy** in Delhi declared that India, like Britain, was now at war with Germany. Gandhi's belief in nonviolence was now stronger than any sense of loyalty he felt to Great Britain, and he opposed any Indian participation in the war. However, most of the other **INC** leaders were prepared to support Britain in exchange for a promise of independence when the war ended.

The British, however, failed to make such a promise, and the majority of Indians slowly turned against them. By 1942, the INC was united behind Gandhi's "Quit India" campaign of **civil disobedience.** When Gandhi was arrested, the country erupted in a series of violent protests.

Family ties

After Gandhi's arrest, Kasturbai spoke at a meeting in his place, and was then sent to Yeravda Prison alongside him. In February 1944, she died in his arms of acute bronchitis while they were both in prison. Their road together may have been rocky at the start, but in later life they had been inseparable.

As a father Gandhi had also improved with age. Gandhi's second son, Manilal, found his father to be much more loving when he returned from South Africa in 1945. Gandhi's younger sons, Ramdas and Devadas, already knew his more affectionate side. One or both of them had been at Gandhi's side throughout the great campaigns of the 1920s and early 1930s.

Independence

Gandhi was released from prison in May 1944. Fifteen months later World War II ended, and new political leaders in Britain were finally ready to speed up India's transition to independence. However, Jinnah's **Muslim League** was now set on achieving **partition**—the division of India into separate **Hindu** and **Muslim** countries—because they did not feel they would be fairly represented in the government of a country that was mainly Hindu. When the British and the INC disagreed with partition, the Muslim League called for direct action. Hindu-Muslim clashes increased in both number and violence, particularly in Bengal and the Punjab.

▲ *Gandhi poses here with Muslim leader Muhammad Jinnah, whom he failed to persuade against partition.*

Gandhi toured many areas promoting peace, but the violence between Hindus and Muslims continued to escalate through 1946 and 1947. Faced with the alternative of a **civil war,** the INC reluctantly decided to accept partition. Gandhi was the only one who refused to believe that the differences between the two groups could not be worked out.

▲ *Bodies litter Chitpore Road in Calcutta after Hindu-Muslim riots in August 1946 resulted in over 3,000 deaths.*

YOU CAN FIND THE PLACES GANDHI TRAVELED IN INDIA ON THE MAP ON PAGE 40.

In July 1947, Britain's **Parliament** passed the Indian Independence Act. This stated that the lines between the new nations of India and Pakistan must be drawn by midnight on August 14, 1947. When the borders were set, millions of people fled their old homes, **Muslims** moving to Pakistan and **Hindus** to India. It was an extremely violent time, and almost one million innocent people were killed in the riots that followed the creation of the two separate nations.

Gandhi refused to join the Independence Day celebrations in Delhi, calling the day a "**spiritual** tragedy." He traveled to the areas that had been most affected by violence in an attempt to bring peace. In January 1948, he once again **fasted** unto death, and once again various leaders sat by his bed and promised to respect the lives and property of other communities. It was his last fast.

Death

In Delhi, Gandhi had concentrated on saving the Muslim minority from the Hindu majority, and some Hindus thought he had betrayed them. Two days after he broke his fast, a Hindu **extremist** was arrested for trying to throw a bomb into Gandhi's daily prayer meeting. "If I fall victim to an assassin's bullet," Gandhi said afterwards, "there must be no anger within me. God must be in my heart and on my lips."

At a prayer meeting on January 30, 1948, another Hindu extremist stepped forward and shot him three times in the stomach and heart. Gandhi collapsed, murmured the words "Oh God," and died.

His body was burned in a traditional Hindu ceremony by the Jumna River, and most of his ashes were scattered at the meeting of the Jumna and Ganges Rivers. Some ashes were given to family and friends, but requests for ashes from around the world had to be refused. In death, as in life, there was not enough of Gandhi to go around.

◀ This photo shows Gandhi with two relatives just one day before his death.

No ordinary light

"The light has gone out of our lives and there is darkness everywhere and I do not quite know what to tell you and how to say it. Our beloved leader, Bapu [father] as we call him, is no more . . . . The light has gone out, I said, and yet I was wrong. For the light that shone in this country was no ordinary light."

(Jawaharlal Nehru, addressing India on the radio on the evening of Gandhi's death, January 30, 1948)

Gandhi played a very important role in winning independence from the British. From the time he returned to India in 1915 through the great **noncooperation** campaigns of the 1920s and 1930s, he not only made it difficult for the British to rule India, he also made them doubt their right to do so. Using original and highly creative plans, he took the moral high ground and proved to the entire world that the British had no right to rule India.

Gandhi also pushed his own countrymen to change. Time and again he forced **Hindus** and **Muslims** to be aware of one another's rights, and he cannot be blamed for the fact that their mutual distrust proved stronger. In a similar way, he forced his fellow Hindus to face the reality of their mistreatment of the **Untouchables,** and for this alone he deserves an honored place in history.

▲ *This statue of Gandhi in the Indian city of Bangalore shows him marching on one of his campaigns.*

Gandhi's use of mass campaigns, which involved the participation of Indians at all levels of society, paved the way for democracy in the postindependence years. In some respects, however, independent India is not exactly what he hoped it would be. Shortly before his death he expressed his hope that India would not become as **materialistic** as Western nations, but under Nehru and successive leaders India has indeed followed an economic development modeled on the Western nations. There has been little development of **cottage industries** in the villages. The **caste** system still affects Indian society, women remain far from equal, and **intercommunal** violence continues to erupt from time to time.

A hard act to follow

In later life Gandhi had a worldwide reputation, and his inspiration has helped others since his death. Martin Luther King Jr., the American civil rights leader, ran his own campaigns against **racial discrimination** as Gandhi did, using "the force of truth" as his only weapon. Tragically, he too was gunned down by the forces of prejudice and ignorance.

Role model

"Gandhi was inevitable. If humanity is to progress, Gandhi is inescapable. He lived, thought, and acted, inspired by a vision of humanity evolving towards a world of peace and harmony. We may ignore him at our risk."

(Martin Luther King Jr.)

In the second half of the twentieth century there were more instances of people following Gandhi's principles. For example, hundreds of nonviolent protests were held against the Vietnam War in the 1960s and 1970s. Despite a belief held by many that Gandhi's nonviolent ways are worth practicing, no major new "Gandhi" has recently risen to prominence in any of the world's long-running conflicts. Many people, however, see echoes of his spirit in the work of exiled Tibetan leader the Dalai Lama.

A force for good

Gandhi may seem to be an old-fashioned figure in some ways, but many of the causes he fought for—**cottage industry,** peaceful change, and a reverence for all life—seem even more important today than they did in his lifetime. In the United States and Great Britain, the increasing interest in small-scale businesses that do not hurt the environment, Eastern religion, animal rights, and **vegetarianism** owes at least something to Gandhi's long-term influence. Many individuals throughout the world are still guided by his ideas and principles.

Above all, Gandhi will be remembered for the example he set. He stood for peace against violence, for **spiritual** fulfillment against the empty satisfactions of greed and **materialism,** and for truth against the comfort of illusions and the evil of lies. When he thought it necessary to prove a point, he put his own life on the line, not the lives of others. He was a good man who moved the world, and was an example to all.

▲ Gandhi's room at the **ashram** in Sevagram was preserved after his death. His few important possessions—prayer beads, glasses, and boxed spinning wheel—lie on the bed.

Epitaph

"The sudden flash of his death revealed a vast darkness. No one who survived him had tried so hard—and with so much success—to live a life of truth, kindness, self-effacement [modesty], humility [humbleness], service, and nonviolence throughout a long, difficult struggle against mighty adversaries [enemies]. He fought passionately and unremittingly [without stopping] against British rule of his country and the evil in his own countrymen. But he kept his own hands clean in the midst of the battle. He fought without malice [ill will] or falsehood or hate."

(American journalist Louis Fischer, who met Gandhi on several occasions)

Timeline

1869	Mohandas Kharamchand Gandhi is born on October 2 in Porbandar, Gujarat.
1883	He marries Kasturbai Makanji.
1885	The **INC** is founded. Gandhi's father dies.
1887	Gandhi finishes school and attends Samaldas College for one term.
1888	His first son, Harilal, is born.
1889	He starts studying law in England.
1892	His second son, Manilal, is born.
1893	Gandhi takes a job in South Africa.
1894	He founds the **Natal Indian Congress.**
1896	He brings wife and sons to South Africa.
1897	His third son, Ramdas, is born.
1899	The **Second Boer War** breaks out. Gandhi forms the Indian Ambulance Corps.
1900	His fourth son, Devadas, is born.
1901	Gandhi returns to India.
1902	He is summoned back to South Africa.
1903	He begins to publish *Indian Opinion*.
1904	He establishes Phoenix Farm.
1907	Gandhi launches his first *satyagraha* campaign.
1910	He establishes Tolstoy Farm.
1913–14	He launches his second *satyagraha* campaign.
1914	He negotiates the Indian Relief Act with J. Smuts. **World War I** starts.
1915	Gandhi returns to India, tours the country, and establishes an *ashram* at Sabarmati.
1916	He speaks at the opening of **Hindu** University in Benares.
1917	He campaigns in Champaran on behalf of **indigo** farmers.

1918	The **Rowlatt Bills** are passed by the British Government.
1919	The *hartal* and the Amritsar Massacre occur.
1920	The **noncooperation** campaign begins.
1922	The Chauri Chaura incident takes place. Gandhi is arrested and imprisoned.
1924	Gandhi **fasts** for Hindu-**Muslim** unity. He is released from prison.
1925–28	Gandhi tours India.
1928	The Simon Commission arrives.
1929	The INC declares Indian independence.
1930	Gandhi opens a new campaign with the Salt March.
1931	He agrees to the Delhi Pact, and travels to England for meetings with the British government.
1932	He is again imprisoned. He fasts for better treatment of **Untouchables.**
1933–39	Gandhi tours India again.
1939	**World War II** starts.
1942	Gandhi leads the "Quit India" campaign. He is arrested and imprisoned.
1944	Kasturbai dies.
1945–47	Violence between Hindus and Muslims increases.
1947	India achieves independence. Gandhi fasts for communal peace in Calcutta.
1948	He fasts for communal peace in Delhi. Gandhi is assassinated on January 30.

Key People of Gandhi's Time

Churchill, Winston Spencer (1874–1965) Churchill was a British politician. During the 1930s Churchill spoke out against the timid policy of successive British governments in both Europe and India. He became **prime minister** during the crucial early phase of **World War II,** and opposed any concessions to Indian **nationalism**, famously declaring that he had "not become the king's first minister in order to preside at the liquidation of the British **Empire**."

Gokhale, Gopal Krishna (1866–1915). This Indian nationalist politician was the leader of the moderates in the **INC** in the years before **World War I.** He much admired the young Gandhi, and expected him to eventually become the leader of India's fight for independence.

Jinnah, Muhammad Ali (1876–1948). Jinnah was an Indian **Muslim** and Bombay lawyer prominent in the **Muslim League** (founded in 1906). In the years following World War I he was friendly to the INC, but after becoming leader of the League in 1934 his overwhelming priority was the protection of Muslim minority interests after independence. Starting in 1937, he campaigned for a separate Muslim state of Pakistan. The turmoil that followed his Direct Action Day in August 1946 persuaded the INC to accept **partition** and the creation of Pakistan. He became the new country's first governor-general in 1947, but died the following year.

Nehru, Jawaharlal (1889–1964). Nehru was an Indian lawyer and politician. He was the son of Motilal Nehru, also a prominent member of the INC. Like Gandhi, Nehru studied law in England. Unlike Gandhi, he was an **agnostic,** a believer in scientific progress, and a **socialist.** Despite these differences there was a strong bond between them. Nehru became involved in the independence struggle in the years following World War I and was imprisoned nine times by the British. He was elected president of the INC in 1929 and announced India's declaration of independence at the end of that year. In 1947 he became prime minister of the newly independent India, a post he held until his death in 1964.

Smuts, Jan (1870–1950). This South African soldier and politician led **Boer** forces during the **Second Boer War.** He later became a leading advocate of Anglo-Boer cooperation, a minister in the colonial administration, and one of the founders of the Union of South Africa (1909). He served as prime minister in the 1930s and played a prominent role in the foundation of both the League of Nations and the United Nations.

Tagore, Rabindranath (1861–1941). This Indian writer and philosopher won the Nobel Prize for Literature in 1913. Knighted in 1915, he gave the honor back after the Amritsar Massacre in 1919. It was he who named Gandhi the *Mahatma* ("the great soul").

Viceroys of India during the struggle for independence

1916–21	Lord Chelmsford	1936–43	Lord Linlithgow
1921–26	Lord Reading	1943–47	Lord Wavell
1926–31	Lord Irwin	1947	Lord Mountbatten
1931–36	Lord Willingdon		

Sources for Further Research

Bains, Rae. *Gandhi, Peaceful Warrior.* Mahwah, N.J.: Troll Communications, 1996.

Fisher, Leonard Everett. *Gandhi.* New York: Atheneum Books for Young Readers, 1995.

Furbee, Mike and Mary Rodd Furbee. *Mohandas Gandhi.* Farmington Hills, Mich.: Gale Group, 2000.

Gandhi, Arun. *Gandhi for Youth.* Memphis, Tenn.: M. K. Gandhi Institute for Nonviolence, 1998.

Ganeri, Anita. *India.* Broomall, Penn.: Chelsea House Publishers, 2000.

Heinrichs, Ann. *Mahatma Gandhi.* Milwaukee, Wisc.: Gareth Stevens, 2001.

Kelly, Nigel, Rosemary Rees, and Jane Shuter. *The Twentieth Century World.* Chicago: Heinemann Library, 1998.

Lazo, Caroline. *Mahatma Gandhi.* Parsippany, N.J.: Silver Burdett Press, 1993.

Malaspina, Ann. *Mahatma Gandhi & India's Independence in World History.* Berkeley Heights, N.J.: Enslow Publishers, 2000.

Park, Ted. *India.* New York: Raintree Steck-Vaughn, 2001.

For further information on Gandhi's life, readers can log on to http://www.mkgandhi.org.

Glossary

agent representative of a company or government

agnostic person who neither believes nor disbelieves in God

artisan skilled craftsperson

ashram home of a group of people dedicated to self-improvement through spiritual means

Bhagavad Gita long poem considered to be one of Hinduism's most important religious texts

Boer South African descended from Dutch settlers

caste social class in Hindu society. There are four main castes: Brahmans (priests and scholars), Kshatriyas (rulers, warriors, and administrators), Vaisyas (farmers and merchants), and Sudras (artisans, laborers, and slaves).

celibacy not having any sexual relationships

civil disobedience peaceful form of protest usually involving the refusal to obey particular laws or to pay particular taxes

civil war war between different groups within one country

commune community in which living space, possessions, and ideas are shared

cottage industry business carried out within the home

cricket game, similar to baseball, played with a bat and ball

dhoti cloth worn around the hips

dominion status self-government within an empire

East India Company British company founded in 1600 to open Asia to British trading. Although its focus was originally on trade, the company later acted in an entirely political manner and paved the way for British domination of India.

empire several countries ruled by the ruler and government of another country. Here, the term refers to the British Empire.

extremist person who believes in extreme political or religious measures

fakir holy man who relies on the charity of others

fast giving up all food for a specific period of time. To fast unto death is to refuse to eat until specific conditions are met or the person fasting dies

hartal planned, widespread strike

Hindu follower of Hinduism, the main religion and social system of India, which traditionally features multiple gods, a belief in reincarnation, and the caste system

home rule government of a country by its own citizens

indentured laborer person who has their passage to a new country, room, and board paid for by an employer, and who then agrees to work for that employer for a certain length of time

Indian Civil Service government jobs that were appointed, not elected, by the British

Indian National Congress (INC) political organization founded in 1885 to discuss increased Indian participation in the country's government

indigo plant from which blue dye is made

industrialism economic system dominated by manufacturing businesses

intercommunal between communities

Islam one of the world's three major monotheistic (one God) religions; founded by the Prophet Mohammed in the seventh century

king-emperor from 1877 to 1947 the British monarch was considered both emperor (or empress) of India and king (or queen) of Britain and the other parts of its empire

lathi bamboo cane with a steel tip

materialism tendency to consider material things such as possessions and physical comforts more important than spiritual values

Muslim follower of Islam

Muslim League political organization founded in 1906 to represent the interests of Indian Muslims

Natal Indian Congress political organization founded by Gandhi in 1894 to represent the interests of Indians in Natal

nationalist person working for the advancement of his or her nation, particularly when there is conflict with the interests of foreign ruling power. Nationalism is the belief in actively working for the advancement of one's nation.

negotiate to work toward agreeing on an outcome

noncooperation in India, a refusal on the part of Indians to do what the British wanted them to do

Parliament governing body, like the U.S. Congress

partition in India, the division of the British-ruled area into the two separate countries of India and Pakistan

petition written request, usually signed by many people

prime minister elected leader of a country, like a president

Prince of Wales man next in line to become King of England

Quakers Christian group devoted to peace

racial discrimination treating people badly because they belong to a particular racial group

Rowlatt Bills group of laws passed by British politicians in India (against the wishes of all Indian representatives) allowing cases to be tried without juries and people to be imprisoned without trials

salvation freeing from ignorance

satyagraha force of truth (*satya* is truth, *agraha* is force)

satyagrahi fighter whose only weapon is the force of truth

Second Boer War war between Great Britain and the two Boer republics of Transvaal and the Orange Free State (1899–1902)

sedition conduct, speech, or writing that encourages rebellion

self-sufficiency providing one's own food, clothing, and shelter

separate electorate system of voting that permits different groups to each vote their own representatives into a political governing body

socialist person who believes the needs of the community should be placed above the needs of the individual

spat piece of cloth that covers the top part of the shoe and the wearer's ankle

spiritual concerned with the world of the spirit rather than the world of material things

Untouchable member of the lowest possible class of Indian society, who does the lowliest, dirtiest jobs

Veda sacred Hindu book of knowledge

vegetarian someone who does not eat meat

viceroy the British government's representative in India

vow solemn promise, often to God

World War I international war involving most European nations as well as Russia, the United States, and countries of the Middle East from 1914 to 1918

World War II international war involving most European nations as well as Russia, the United States, Japan, and China from 1939 to 1945

Index